GOD'S GIFT OF POETRY

Poems Sent from the King

By Maria Tipton

GOD'S GIFT OF POETRY

To be a mother is not an easy task,
yet you do it proudly everyday no matter what is asked.
You have turned your baby into a beautiful young lady.
You were there for me since the beginning and saved me countless tears.
The pushy and wise advice you gave will carry me through the years.
With my every mistake or wrongful deed,
you were always there to understand.
You never forget to say you care or that you love me too.
There is no other person that will shape my heart the way you've done,
your job finished perfectly for your precious daughters and sons.
We have had a rocky road through triumph and catastrophe, hard time and despair,
but not a single moment of time of not having a wonderful mother there.
I know that my teen years have driven you crazy but you have guided me with assurance along the way.
You have given me comfort and certainty with every breath I take within the day.
Your little girl is growing up but your baby girl will always remain deep inside me.
There are not enough words that can thank you for everything you have helped me emotionally and physically.

GOD'S GIFT OF POETRY

I have my future ahead of me and you are the women that has led me and guided me towards the proper path. No other person deserves a more wonderful mother than from me to you.

Love your baby girl,
Bridgette Montgomery

My mother is such a loving and caring person, with a wonderful sense of humor and a great big heart. She has been this way all her life. It is no surprise to me that God would bless her to put encouraging words on to paper for others to read and to be encouraged and instructed by. Maria Tipton is an extreme blessing, and my best friend too! I pray that everyone that picks the book up will be bless by the words that the Holy Spirit instructed her to write!

Your daughter
Gena

My mother is so beautiful. Her spiritual poetry has helped me along my journey in life. She is such an inspiration to my life. I love her so much. I am so blessed and so proud that she is my mother. I Love Her Dearly!

Lisa Savage

GOD'S GIFT OF POETRY

To my sister, who I love for being such a blessing in my life. Full of joy and peace. Read her works and be blessed also. That I am sure of.

Jack Dunbar

This is a dedication to my dear sister Maria whom I am so blessed and proud to call her not just my sister but my best friend also. I've watched Maria throughout her years of devoting her time, energy and love to serve the Lord which so much joy giving her whole heart to Him. The Lord has blessed you my dear sister with the gift of writing and sharing these beautiful words in the form of poetry. His anointing is with you, on you and around you. Keep being the strong woman of God has chosen you to be. There is so much more I can say and share but there isn't enough words and room to put it all down. I love you Maria and am so very blessed to call you my sister. Love you so much Maria.

Charlene Head

Beauty
Beauty is a word that symbolizes a person or a thing that rings joy and happiness to you. The most beautiful aspect in my life is my mom, she embodies the concept of beauty to me. As a child my mom always went the extra mile to ensure that we were cared for and loved. She gave us security and peace, when life gave her challenges she gave us grace and comfort. That's Beauty! She made us laugh and cry on the facts of life, she is an inspiration to us and more importantly to me with her tenacity and perseverance to keep moving forward in a positive and

productive manner.

Beauty to me is my mom! My mother has always been artistic from as far back as I can remember, from her clay figurines to her poetry to her tote garden and the list goes on and on. She inspired me to be who I am, I love mom and thank you and more importantly I thank God for giving a special mother to me. God has always been with you and it is relevant in your poetry and how you express yourself to others. That's Beauty! That's my mom. I love you.

Greg Rhodes

Evangelist Maria Tipton is one who loves the Lord and is a devoted faithful loving lady of God. She is faithful to both God and her husband which I am happy to be. She has truly been a great companion and a blessing full of words of exaltation, confrontation, and consultation messages sent from the Most High God. She's on fire for Jesus and a true warrior for the Lord Jesus Christ. Her poetry flows like rivers of living water!

Lovingly,
Your Husband, Elder, Robert M. Tipton

GOD'S GIFT OF POETRY

Copyright © Maria Tipton, December 25, 2015

No part of this book may be reproduced by any means, electronic or written, without the written permission of the author.

All scriptures are from the KJV of the Bible.

All Rights Reserved.

God's Gift of Poetry
Written by
Maria Tipton

ISBN 9780692586990

Library of Congress

Dayspring Touch Press
2127 Doctor's Park Drive
Columbus, IN 47203

Dedication

Special thanks to my wonderful mother, Helen Louise Gordon for teaching me to never give up, to love regardless of who they were and how to survive. She was a hard working woman. I can see her now with her long black coat on, walking in snow up to her knees. She always held her head slightly to one side and her shoulder straight and tall. Her hands would be so cold, she would cry as she placed them in water.

GOD'S GIFT OF POETRY

In 1940 times were very pressing but my mother gave me the best of everything. I remember on Christmas she would have so much under my tree. She would take me to the best clothing store for my school clothes. I am so amazed at how she struggled to give me the best.

She told me if I passed to the second grade she would buy me a bike. Well I passed and she bought me a brand new bike. I thank you mother for the wonderful thing you did for me. I am so thankful to God that you and I were able to be together in your latter years. I convinced her to get on an airplane, we went to California with our church. She was so precious, her eyes got very big as the plane took off and she just smiled. She was a wonderful woman and will always be in my heart. I praise God she gave her life to Christ and enjoyed the power of the Holy Ghost. Thank you Mother.

Maria Tipton

Special Thanks and Acknowledgments

Although I have been inspired to write the poems as they came, this book was not a singular effort. Bishop Anthony Pippens allowed me to read a poem I had written to the congregation during service. He liked the poem so much that he requested I write a poem for every Sunday and put in the church programs. I was so grateful to God because He blessed me to write a poem for every Sunday. I truly thank Bishop Pippens for his support and encouragement. Because of his request I have written many poems.

I also acknowledge Pastor Frank Griffin. He is responsible for setting up my appointment with Dayspring Touch Press Publishers because he thought my poems should be published.

Thank you Pastor Griffin.

Foreword

There are many things I could say about Maria Tipton. She is a mother, a wife, a retired nurse of 30 years and an experienced worker in the Kingdom of God. She has held several positions in the church including Prison Ministry, Nursing Home and Hospital Ministry, Homeless & Bereavement, Sunday School Teacher and Preacher. But above all those things, I know Maria Tipton as one who loves people.

She displayed that love on her job, and because of that love, she was nominated, in 1986, as Nurse of the year at St Francis Hospital in Beech Grove, Indiana.

I believe it is that same love for people that gave birth to this book of poems. Poetry covers a very important section of the word of God. Five Books, (Job, Psalms, Proverbs, Ecclesiastes and Song of Solomon) make up the books of poetry in the Bible. From the dramatic suffering of Job to the poetic love song in the Song of Solomon, poetry has a very significant place in the Kingdom of God.

GOD'S GIFT OF POETRY

Clearly gifted with insight and words, the authors of these poetic books don't just tell stories, but paint pictures in our hearts and in our minds of the highs and lows of our walk with God. Maria Tipton has that gift. Maria Tipton has that insight. She can see a current event and transform it, through words, into an emotional connection that did not exist before. Experience might not be the best teacher, but it is a very good teacher, and Maria has gleaned from life's experiences, allowing her to see the world, like many other great poets, in a unique and very expressive way.

"When I see Maria or talk to Maria, I can tell she cares for me and whatever I am talking about. She is such a loving person. And for her, love is an action word, and she shows it every day. It could be a quick call to tell me she was praying for me or a hug in church during our visitors welcoming. Her focus seems to be to show God's love wherever she goes". Those are the words from my wife Debra Griffin, describing her experiences with Evangelist Maria Tipton; A woman who walks in love. That love of God and love for God's people shines throughout this book. The interplay with words speak to her gift of intellect. The relevance of her statements speak to her wisdom, but her emotional connection and empathetic approach speak to her gift of love.

It will be the loving connection that will overpower you and will set this work apart from others. As you look for that empathic voice of reason and understanding you will find yourself revisiting sections of this book, which hit closer to home. This will be a common occurrence. For that purpose I am honored and have the great privilege of introducing this work to the world. As you read, take your time, digest and don't miss your blessing.

Dr. Frank J. Griffin
Pastor,
Thy Kingdom Come Ministries

Contents

God's Gift of Poetry	1
Dedication	7
Special Thanks and Acknowledgments	9
Foreword	10
INTRODUCTION	15
CHAPTER 1	18
CHAPTER 2	28
CHAPTER 3	38
CHAPTER 4	43
CHAPTER 5	50
CHAPTER 6	62
Conclusion	83
Index	92

GOD'S GIFT OF POETRY

INTRODUCTION

<u>What Time Is It</u>

As I look around and see all the hatred and pain.
A lot of people looking as though they are Insane.

Sitting in a prayer meeting and packing a gun.
Killing innocent people and take off and run.

Little babies are beaten to death.
Evil looking at them as they take their last breath.

People all over the world, hungry and not being fed.
Evil torturing people, even cutting off heads.

People sleeping in the streets, lying on the ground.
There are many empty buildings all around.

Many false prophets telling lies.
Making you think they are so wise.

Jesus The Master, is going to come, like a thief in the night.
Evil, you are going to be removed clean out of sight.

Your time is coming to an end you ungodly liar.
You are going to be cast into the Lake Of Fire.

GOD'S GIFT OF POETRY

Scripture Reference Revelation 20:10

GOD'S GIFT OF POETRY

CHAPTER 1

<u>CONTRARY</u>

Where is the mind of man going?
There is no warmth, compassion or love showing.

I see teenagers on the street late at night:
They are looking and searching for someone to fight.

I hear the universal cry of a child:
People all around them shooting and acting wild.

A child in the yard playing a game;
A blast from a gun kills them or they are maimed.

A man standing on the corner his body racking with pain;
His guts churning, wanting, needing that terrible cocaine.

A line on the street marching and protesting;
The law is releasing men who have been molesting.

Man wanting to be woman and a woman wanting to be a man;
A child suffering physical abuse from a parent's hand.

Unborn child not given a chance of life;

GOD'S GIFT OF POETRY

Homes everywhere full of anger and strife.

Obscene music blasting into ears everywhere;
No one has respect or even cares.

Listen! My dear brothers and sisters, haven't you heard;
All these actions are contrary to God's holy word.

The King James Study Bible Scripture:
Galatians 5:19-21

*19How the works of the flesh are
manifest, which are these; Adultery,
fornication, uncleanness, lasciviousness,
20Idolatry, witchcraft, hatred, variance,
emulations, wrath, strife, seditions, heresies,
21Envyings, murders, drunkenness, revelling,
and such like: of the which I tell you before, as I have also told
you in time past, that they which do such things shall not
inherit the kingdom of God.*

FREE

JESUS IS EVERYTHING TO ME;
HE IS THE ONE WHO SET ME FREE,

I WAS BOUND IN A WORLD OF SIN;
FIGHTING A BATTLE A BATTLE I COULDN'T WIN.

WONDERING WHERE DO I GO FROM HERE;
LAUGHING TO HIDE MY FEAR.

REACHING OUT AND THERE IS NO ONE THERE;
REALIZING THAT NO ONE CARES.

THEN I HEARD ABOUT A MAN WHO ALWAYS SEES US;
THIS MAN IS CALLED JESUS.

HE IS THE ONE WHO DIED ON THE CROSS;
SO THAT OUR SOULS WOULDN'T BE LOST.

SINCE I HAVE COME TO KNOW THIS MAN;
I STAND UP AND SHOUT VICTORY AND WAVE MY HANDS.

I AM OUT OF THE DARK NOW AND IN A SPIRITUAL LIGHT;
I AM SINGING SONGS OF PRAISE NOW AND PRAYING FOR SPIRITUAL FLIGHT.

WHO IS THIS MAN WHO KNOWS ALL THINGS?
THIS MAN IS JESUS OUR HEAVENLY KING.

He Is Risen

Jesus has risen from the dead! Glory Hallelujah! We are now covered under His precious blood that He shed.

The curtain is now ripped from the top to the bottom and the way is clear.
You can now go straight to the Master, have no fear.

We were once in darkness, burden in sin.
Because of His death, burial, resurrection and the Holy Ghost, we are going to win.

I love you my Holy King who came from above.
I am so grateful for your holy and unconditional love.
Your Holy presence is of an infinite magnitude.
I bow down before you with humbleness and great gratitude.

It is certainly not over, there is more to come.
I know you are going to do what you said you would do, this I surely know.

For you said in John 14:3 And if I go and prepare
a place for you, I will come again, and receive
you unto myself, that where I am ye may be also.

GOD'S GIFT OF POETRY

This is why I am so excited and determined to win this spiritual battle, by your mercy and grace.

For when it is all over, I'll be able to look upon thy face.

Seeking

Lord I am seeking you hour by hour and day by day.
I know only you Jesus will show me the right way.
I want to be your vessel full of knowledge and delight.
I want to be your soldier ready to serve in this spiritual fight.
I want to spread the love you so graciously gave.
When you hung on the cross so that we could be saved.
I thank you Jesus for your grace and power.
You are truly the king who sets in the heavenly high tower.
I praise you, I glorify your name. It is victory, victory that I shall claim.

The King

Behold a star in the heavens shined bright.
Casting down upon Bethlehem, its glorious light.

A wondrous birth had just occurred. Even the shepherds abiding in the fields, had heard.

Wrapped in swaddling cloth and lying in a manger.
His precious life would soon be in danger.

Behold this precious babe grew into a man.
He went around preaching teaching and healing with his hand.

He preached the word to all that would listen.
He tried to teach the so called Christians.

Sometimes he had nowhere to lay his head.
He so awesomely raised Lazarus from the dead.

There were twelve who followed him everywhere he went.
There was one who betrayed him for coins that were never spent.

They beat him with a whip that ripped his flesh to pieces.
This is what they did to my sweet Jesus!

They shoved a crown of thorns upon his head.
Causing deep wounds that bled and bled.

They laid him down on a cross and nailed to it his hands and feet.
Oh no! his suffering is not yet complete.

They crucified him so another could be set free.
What a terrible thing to do, they just wouldn't believe!

They pierced him in his side and the blood and water came running through.
He said, "Father forgive them for they know not what they do."

Well, you see the Pharisees thought they had won but they didn't win. This great and holy King said in St John 10:18 No man taketh it from me, but I lay it down myself. I have power to lay it down, and I have power to take it up again.

WOMAN

I am a woman created by God's hand.
I was made from the rib of a man.

I am gentle, soft, bold and strong.
You can count on me when things go wrong.

I have been in a struggle for many years.
Sometimes working so hard until I am in tears.

Raised in a world of sin and oppression.
Fighting my fears and unwanted depression.

Here I am now, with the help of Jesus continuing to be strong in this fight, not forgetting that Jesus is my light.

I will forge ahead and not look back.
For I am a woman that God colored black.

GOD'S GIFT OF POETRY

CHAPTER 2

<u>A YEAR BY GRACE</u>

His Grace has brought me through another year, again.
I have been wondrously loved, protected, comforted, fed, clothed, kept free and forgiven of my sins.

My prayer is that I was able to take a step up on heaven's ladder.
I have learned, bless God. All the material things just don't matter.

My eternal spirit has become my priority.
It's all about Jesus now and certainly not of me.

As the grapes age to make fine wine.
Well I have aged another year because of the great Divine.

I am excited about the year ahead.
I will not look back but my direction is to the kingdom instead.

My days are numbered, how many I don't know.
My desire *is* when Jesus comes I can go.

GOD'S GIFT OF POETRY

As I complete this God given poem expressing how I feel.
I know whatever will be, will be God's will.

So Happy New Year my dear ones! May God bless you each and every day.
And always remember Jesus Christ is the only way.

Comforter

I know some of your pain and sorrow;
But I must tell you, there is hope on tomorrow.

Just take one day at a time and don't try to reach for more;
Know that the comforter is at your side and will give that emotional peace you are searching for.

The Lord will bless you with emotional peace;
His mercy and grace will never cease.

He will eventually fill that voided space;
He will drape you with his love and grace.

So take care my dear ones, don't be afraid;
Sweet Jesus will carry you all the way.

HEAVEN

No more pain, no more sorrow;
No more concerns about tomorrow.

Joy in the air, songs of praise;
Endless time not counted as days.

Timeless beauty before your eyes;
Away beyond the clear blue skies.

Wondrous feeling of perfect peace;
All are equal, none counted as least.

All the old is a thing of the pass;
Everything brand new and shall forever last.

RUNNING CHILD

Where is that dear sweet child?
Are they out of control and running wild?

What has happened and what went wrong?
Not enough love, not enough respect, not enough
guidance and not enough spiritual unity, Yes! And for
too long.

This is the end result, can't you see;
Neglecting our children and letting them run free.

It is time to reach out!
Let them know what love, guidance, respect and most of
all, what JESUS is all about!

It is time to take a Stand!
Reach out, take that child in hand.

Let your voice be heard, say it loud;
It is time to stop the running child!

THE MATTERS OF THE HEART

The matters of the heart come from deep within.
If you are not careful they enter most parts of your heart will cause you to sin.

A person may demonstrate to be pure and holy on the external side.
Thinking they have fooled others with their deception of lies.

You see, the matters of the heart go beyond the anatomy.
Remember, all things God knows and all things He sees.

I believe it is time to check where we stand.
Is our heart directed by God or are we following man.

The heart is the director of our mind.
Pray tell, what thoughts do you have that God will find.

If you have not taken thought of these things, I suggest this is the time to start.

Proverbs 21:2 *Every way of a man is right in his own eyes, but the Lord pondereth the hearts.*

THE SUFFERING

The Master draped himself in the flesh of a man.
His presents on this earth was in His holy plan.

He knew his suffering would be of a great magnitude.
He did it because of his great love for me and you.

The Jews had been waiting for many years for the
Messiah to appear on the scene.
But when he did they were hostile and mean.

After He was betrayed by a kiss and coins never spent.
He knew time was near for the atonement.

There were about 500 to 1200 soldiers that spat on Him
until it was dripping from His skin.
His flesh was ripped and torn as they beat Him with a
whip over and over again.

Now remember He was in the flesh like you and me.
He was feeling all the excruciating pain and misery.

They made a crown of thorns about an inch and a half
long and shoved it down on the Master's head.
Where the thorns dug deep the Master bled and bled.

He was pushed, shoved and kicked all around.
He was forced to carry the heavy cross that burdened
Him to the ground.

They nailed Him to the cross with large spikes through one hand then the other and one through His feet.
Now there is more for His suffering, was not yet complete.

Remember, a sword had also pierced Him in His side.
He hung there on the cross and the ninth hour Jesus cried out with a loud voice, Eli, Eli lama sabachthani!

His mouth was parched and so very dry and He was given vinegar to drink.
I know these words are painful to hear but I wrote them this way to make people think.

Now you would think after all this terrible suffering His voice would be a whisper at most.
But our Lord and Savior Cried out again with a loud voice and gave up the Ghost.

The sound of His powerful cry, caused the earth to shake and the rocks to rent.
I thank you my precious Savior for glorious love that allows us to bow before you and repent.

Now in conclusion, I must say all those non-believers, they didn't take the Master's life, they didn't win.

Scripture **John 10:18.** *Christ said no man taketh it from me, but I lay it down of myself. I have power to take it again.*

FAREWELL

This is a day of a very sad farewell;
But I know what ever course you take, you will excel.

People come and go;
But you have been a Joy and pleasure to know.

I thank you for all the hugs and support you gave to me during my very difficult days;
I pray a multitude of blessings are headed your way.

Take care and continue to let your light shine:
And always remember all things are possible through the great Divine.

GOD'S GIFT OF POETRY

CHAPTER 3

<u>HE WHO</u>

He who formed a *man* out of the dust;
The very same one I will trust.

He who caused rain for 40 days and 40 nights;
The very same one causes me to go to higher heights.

He who parted the Red Sea;
The very same one is mindful of me.

He who manifested himself into the flesh of a man;
The very same gave me a chance to share his eternal heavenly plan.

He who healed the sick, the blind, mend the lame;
The very same one took me out of a world of shame.

He who rose Lazarus from the dead;
This very same one tells me I am under His Blood he shed.

He who has no beginning or end;

The very same one left his word that tell me how to win.

He who give me strength and power to accomplish my spiritual endeavors;

The very same one "Is the same yesterday and today and forever".

Life

A cell divides and multiplies.
A shape is formed, one that can't be denied.
A tiny heart begins to beat.
Pumping precious blood from head to feet.
The stages of development have come to an end.
This beautiful new life begins to descend.
I took a breath in and my soul stirred within my flesh.
I cried out as I was laid on my mother's breast.
Born in a world depending on guidance and love.
Life was given this babe from Christ above.

LOVE

Take your brother and sister in hand;
It's time to love our fellow man.

God created us all equal, no respect of person;
His commandments instructs us to love one another and this is for certain.

Loving should be our way of life;
Get rid of the prejudice, anger and strife.

I'm so thankful God doesn't feel the way we do;
If he did he would love me and not you, (mmmmm)

It's time to open our hearts and let the love flow;
You may change a mind, you just never know.

GOD'S GIFT OF POETRY

CHAPTER 4

<u>AWAKENED</u>

I awakened this morning with great delight;
I knew another day with Jesus was in sight.

I feel his holy presence, I know I am not alone;
He has touched my very spirit and made his presence known.

It is so wonderful, starting my day with Jesus;
I know he is ever present and will never leave us.

All you have to do is reach out;
He is right there for you, have no doubt.

Please don't start another day without the king;
I guarantee your day will joyful, your mind at peace, and you will be able to overcome many troublesome things.

ETERNAL

Darker than the blackest night;
A place of no peace, contentment, your soul always in an eternal fight.

The stench of death penetrating the thick, damp air;
There are indescribable horrors everywhere.

Evil surrounding you, torturing your soul over and over again;
This is the place that you go to when you die in sin.

Creatures creeping, slimy things moving to and fro; Your soul wants to run but there is no place to go.

Your soul cries out, LORD! LORD! There is no answer to be heard;
If only you had obeyed God's holy word.

For those of you who are not saved, it's not too late;
Don't ponder too long for your soul will be cast into the fiery lake.

Revelation 21:8

FORGIVENESS

WHEN SOMEONE HAS HURT US IN A VENDICT1VE WAY;
WE FEEL BAD BUT THIS IS WHAT WE SHOULD SAY,
MAY THE LORD BLESS AND SHOW THEM THE RIGHT WAY.

I KNOW THIS IS NOT ALL WE MUST DO;
ACCORDING TO GOD'S WORD WE MUST LOVE THEM TOO.

WHO ARE WE THAT WE CANNOT FORGIVE;
FOR THIS IS THE REASON WE ARE ALLOWED TO LIVE.

WE HAVE NO RIGHT TO JUDGE ANYONE FOR THE FAULTS ARE THE WAY THEY ARE LIVING;
DEAR SWEET CHRIST JESUS DIED SO THAT OUR SINS COULD BE FORGIVEN.

WE MUST EXTEND THE LOVE THAT CHRIST SO GRACIOUSLY GAVE;
IT TRULY WAS HIS LOVE THAT CAUSE ME TO BE SAVED.

GALATIANS 6: 1-5 MATTHEW 7: 1-5

HATRED

Hatred is a cancer of the mind;

It will devour and destroy you in time.

If you think hating someone is all right;

Well, think again, come out of the darkness into the light.

Peace is something you will never find;

Because that hate you have, has caused you to be blind.

Open up those eyes and see;

GOD'S word is what you need.

Scripture Reference: **1 John 2:9-11**

MERCY

M is for the MASTER who forgives all our sins;
E is for EVERLASTING, everlasting and forever no end.
R is for the glorious RESURRECTION of our Lord and Savior, Jesus Christ;
C is for the COMFORTER he left behind after his sacrifice.
Y is for "Yea, though I walk through the valley of the shadow of death, I will fear no evil: for thou art with me; thy rod and thy staff they comfort me." "Thou preparest a table before me in the presence of mine enemies: thou anointest my head with oil; my cup runneth over." "Surely goodness and MERCY shall follow me all the days of my life: and I will dwell in the house of the Lord forever."

Thank you Jesus
Scripture reference: **Psalms 23:4-6**

MOTIVATION

What does motivation really mean?
It means believing and trusting in God whom you have never seen.

Praising Him, uplifting His holy name.
Which will most definitely bring about a glorious change.

Make a joyful noise unto the lord all ye lands.
This is guaranteed to make you stand.

To be motivated, you must know the force that motivates.
So read and study the word, for Christ's sake.

The more you know about Him the better you will feel.
And soon His will, will be your will.

Scripture **Matt. 6:33** says *"But seek ye first the kingdom of God and his righteousness: and all these things shall be added unto you."* So if you need motivation, God knows these are the things you should do.

GOD'S GIFT OF POETRY

CHAPTER 5

QUESTION & ANSWERS

Are you tired, always searching but never finding peace, trouble always in the way?

St John 14:27 *Peace I leave with you my peace I give, not as the world giveth give I unto you, let not your heart be troubled, neither let it be afraid.*

Are you lost in a world of sin, always miserable always in an emotional fight?

Matthew 11:2.8-30 *Come unto me all ye that labor and are heavy laden and I will give you rest. Take my yoke upon you and learn of me: for I meek and lowly in heart and ye shall find rest unto your souls. For my yoke is easy and my burden is light.*

Are you always searching for and wanting the ultimate love from someone?

John. 3:16 *For God so loved the world that he gave his only begotten son.*

Are you fearful death will consume you in this terrible world of sin and strife?

St John 6:47 *Verily, verily I say unto you he that believeth on me hath everlasting life.*

Are you tired being manipulated by the evil one in all you do?

James 4:7 *Submit yourselves therefore to God. Resist the devil and, he will flee from you*

So my dear ones you have heard the questions and answers, I pray you will drop your barrier of resistance.

II Peter 3:9 *The Lord is not slack concerning his promise as some men count slackness: but is longsuffering to us ward, not willing that any should perish, but that all should come to repentance.*

Rock A Bye

Rockabye saints the world and all;
When the wind blows will you fall?

Rockabye saints, are you awake;
Will you be left when God comes to take?

Rockabye saints, are you asleep;
For Satan wants your soul for to keep.

Rockabye saints the world and all;
Where will you be when the fire and brimstone falls?

Rockabye saints, please won't you awake;
Sleeping now is a terrible mistake.

Please don't be rocked by Satan's tune;
For Jesus is coming very soon.

Scripture Reference:
Romans 13:11 *and that knowing the time, that now is high time to awake out of sleep: for now is our salvation nearer than when we believe.* **I Thessalonians 5:6** *Therefore let us not sleep as others; but let us watch and be sober.*

SECRET PLACE

When I am surrounded by the terrors of darkness and the way doesn't seem, clear;
I turn to my Savior Jesus for he removes all my fears.

When the enemy comes to attack me on all sides;
I know there is nothing that the enemy can do to me for he is full of lies.

No matter what comes before me I shall be strong;
For God's angels surround me all the day long.

I will trust and abide in his holy word, to him I will forever cling; It is so wonderful here in this secret place, under the shelter of God's wings.

Scripture Reference: **Psalm 91**

SOLDIER

Here comes the enemy straight ahead;
I am full of God's power and I am going to knock him dead.

I got my breastplate on and ready to fight;
My strength comes from God's awesome might.

If we band together as one in love;
We can conquer all things through Christ above.

The wisdom of God has made me bolder;
I am so thankful to be able to say. "I am one of God's soldiers"!

Scripture Reference: **Ephesians 6: 10 - 19**

The Flesh

It is dead and has no good end;
It gets you in trouble and causes you to sin.

It is lustful and unclean;
It will cause you to be disrespectful and mean.

It will lead you into to strife and seduction;
It will guide your self-esteem to total reduction.

Listen to the Spirit which dwelleth within;
The Spirit will help keep you from the turmoil's of sin.

Scripture Reference **Galatians 5:16-25**

Thank You Jesus!

GOD'S GIFT OF POETRY

The Key

The world is a trap, full of sin.
It is ruled by the demons within.

There is no light, just darkness everywhere.
If you notice, those in the dark don't seem to care.

The world will lure you in with deceptions of pleasures.
Offering cocaine, alcohol, crack, lust of the flesh and causing you to ignore all conflictions. Not caring that your end result is hard core addiction.

You have been tricked by the evil one.
Now there is no pleasure no more fun.

Now Satan has trapped you in his world of sin.
He is waiting for your life to end.

"Your soul is what he is waiting for.
Waiting at hell's open door.

I am a former victim of the world, where Satan thought my life was his to take.
But someone told me about the key that would allow me to escape.

I took the key which set me free.
And now I am out of the world of misery.

The key is there for all of us.
The precious key is our Lord and Savior Jesus.

The Stand

My emotions and my heart became overwhelmed as I
saw more than one million black brothers standing
proud and free;
I saw my brothers standing firm on the changes we need.

Fathers for our children, husbands for the wives and
strong spiritual leader for the community;
Giving love, respect and the power of their unity.

I pray this stand is not just for a day;
But for eternity according to God's way.

I hope and pray this great moment will not be in vain;
Because of any one person seeking power and fame.

If all the brothers seek God as their leader in life;
Then this one million stand will be worth all that has
been sacrificed.

This day will be marked down in history.
As the black brother has seen what he can be.

TO GOD BE THE GLORY

Scripture Reference
Philippians 4:13 *I can do all things through Christ who strengthened me.*

THE VERY SAME ONE

He who formed a man out of the dust;
The very same one I will trust.

He who caused rain for 40 days and 40 nights;
The very same one causes me to go to higher heights.

He who parted the Red Sea;
The very same one is mindful of me.

He who manifested himself into the flesh of a man;
The very same gave me a chance to share his eternal heavenly plan.

He who healed the sick, the blind and the lame;
The very same one took me out of a world of shame.

He who rose Lazarus from the dead;
This very same one tells me I am under the blood he shed.

He who has no beginning or end;
The very same one left his word to tell me how to win.

He who gives me strength and power to accomplish my spiritual endeavors;
The very same one is "Jesus Christ, the same yesterday, today, and forever.

TOMORROW

Tomorrow is a day that may be too late;
Putting it off may be a definite mistake.

Things of tomorrow are not promised can't you see?
It is best to do it today and let Christ take the lead.

There will be a day when you won't have a choice;
So listen, listen to that inner voice.

God's promise to those who choose him is eternal life;
What a promise! Do you really have to think twice?

Mother's Love

The love of a mother is so emotionally deep.
Her heart is so precious, her love we so seek.

Such a responsibility she has to keep herself strong.
So that her directive care will embrace you all the day long.

She is not to be taken for granted for all the things she will do.
She does them because of her endearing love for you.

Her work is never done.
Caring for her daughters and sons.

Her fortitude and strength comes from the Lord above.
There is nothing to compare to a good mother's love.

To the mothers living and to those who have passed away.
We honor you, we love you and thank you on this beautiful Mother's Day.

Ephesians 6:2-3
2..Honor thy Father and Mother, which is the first commandment with promise.
3..That it may be with thee, and thou mayest live long on the earth.

GOD'S GIFT OF POETRY

CHAPTER 6

LOVE LETTER TO MY CHILDREN

My dear ones, how I love you.

Each of you are like a gem, precious, beautiful
like dancing lights radiating in my heart.

Remembering your tiny faces, expressions so dear
and unforgettable.

I thank God, that you are a part of my life and of me.

I shall always hold you close within my heart, with
joy and thankfulness.

Now all of you are walking tall, young men and women.
My children, my children!

A proud mother of you I shall always be and may God be
with you.

From Your Loving Mother

Mother

A soft hand and a gentle touch;
A sense of warmth and security means so much.

A stern word to put me in my place;
It was her who taught me to say grace.

She is a queen to me;
Without her presence I wouldn't be.

She is a precious gift from above;
I am so thankful to have my mother's love.

GOD'S GIFT OF POETRY

TKC

Father, How great is thy name in all the earth!
By your grace and mercy TKC was birthed.

Our Pastor and First Lady, sought your will all the way.
This is why we are celebrating TKC's anniversary today.

TKC's foundation is built on unity and love.
The formulary is from God's written word inspired from above.

TKC is a loving, caring church, reaching out to heal, to build up, to comfort, to embrace and giving guidance based on God's kingdom building plan.
We are so blessed to be led by Pastor Frank Griffin. He is humble, caring, loving, intellectual and truly God's chosen man.

Our First Lady, Debra is a strong woman in her faith, she's quiet and determined to be there for her man.
She was chosen by God to be the First Lady because He knew Pastor would need her to complete his plan.

So we thank Jesus for letting us live and see!
This day TKC celebrates our 4th anniversary!

GOD'S GIFT OF POETRY

The Beginning

In the beginning, there was a house not great in size but small;
In this little house, was a family of six and the head of the family had answered God's call.

The little house was fixed up and together with their diligence, faith, hard work and love;
They made the foundation God above.

Husband and wife working side by side;
Letting the Lord be their guide.

Now the Little house was not just a house but a church of a specialty;
It was the beginning of the Pippen's ministry.

They made sacrifices great and small;
They were talked about, back stabbed and some even laughed at them;
But they continued forging ahead, knowing God was at the helm.

There were days of disappointments, hurt and pain;
But they continued on by God's grace, just the same.

Yes! They continued on. God always giving them strength to cope;
Oh! By the way, this little church is Greater New Hope.

Now the Little church began to grow in size;

Because the preacher was chosen of God, he was and is very wise.

He began to have a vision of a bigger church across the street;
Well you guessed right, that vision became reality and that church is complete.

Now they continue to work hard side by side, continuing to do God's will;
Well, Pastor has another vision and I know it too will be fulfilled.

Thru their hard work and faith in God, Elder and Sister Pippens have earned the ultimate respect;
Oh by the way, our Elder is now Bishop Elect.

The little church across the street, well it no longer stands;
It is the parking lot for the member's cars, & vans.

That little church will always have a place in my heart;
For that is where I got my spiritual start.

A LIGHT

A light shines bright, reflecting all that is good within its glow;
A light cannot hide, everyone sees and knows.

A light will make your day full of joy and hope;
A light will give you strength to cope.

Theresa you are a light that always shines;
You have been blessed by the great Divine.

So Theresa, have a great and blessed Birthday:
And let your light shine always.

God's Blessings Always

APPRECIATE

Appreciate, what does this actually mean?
Well, It means, be grateful for, regard highly, value
properly and rise in value, now these are not my
definitions but are from the dictionaries I have seen.

Being grateful for is truly what I am for having spiritual
leadership as Elder and his wife.
Regard highly, I certainly do, for they are loving, kind
and always give good advice.

Value properly is for certain, I respect them and will do
whatever I can to make their load light.
Elders preaching of the true word of God is preparing
me for the heavenly flight.

Rise in value is certainly what they have done.
Their value has risen because of their diligent work
for God and the souls they have won.

Now, I saw another word in the dictionary as I was
thumbing through.
This other word is love, so as I close this God given
poem, I will tell you both with great admiration, I love
you.

FIRST LADY

She is the wife of our pastor and always at his side;
She is always available if a sister needs to confide.

She is a mother with many things to do;
She always wants to know what she can do for you.

She sets a prime example to be proud of;
Her walk and talk are of Christ above.

She does all she can to make Pastor's load light;
She is strong in the word of God for a spiritual fight.

Her duties are endless but she continues to do all she can;
Her unity with elder was truly in God's plan.

She always thanks the Lord for helping her to cope;
This First Lady is Sister Cynthia Pippens of Greater New Hope.

Scripture Reference: **Proverbs 31: 11-31**

MESSAGE

Being a leader of the sheep is not easy to do.
Be encouraged for God is truly with you.

Have no doubt, he is right at your side.
He choose you because he knew, in you his words would abide.

People can be cruel, selfish and don't try to understand.
Pray for them and continue to be God's holy man.

SHOULDN'T BE

I woke up Sunday morning preparing to hear
God's word;
I pulled up in front of the church and saw something that
caused me to be greatly disturbed.

Could this be what my eyes do see?
Is that our Pastor cutting weeds?

I guess it is not enough for him to feed our souls with
God's word several times a week;
Now he has to work at keeping the church grounds neat.

If we did this according to God's plan;
We should be doing all that we can by giving Pastor a
helping hand.

Saying I love you Pastor is alright;
But we must get into action to make his job light.

Some may not like what this poem has to say;
That's too bad it is said anyway.

Alexis

Alexis is strong and I know she can take it; I believe her mind will allow her to make it.

She'll set that dream in her head;
She can make it a reality instead.

Alexis, walk tall and always be proud;
Say, "I can! I can! And say it loud"

You have the greatest on your side;
He loves you so much, for you and I he died.

I'll tell you, Jesus is his name;
Put him in your life and I guarantee you will never be the same.

Another Year

Another year has gone by;
That saying is so true, "How time does fly."

The book of life remains open, another page has been turned;
Time has passed and many lessons learned.

You may not think as fast or remember like you used to;
But thank God you are able to do and go through!

One day your deteriorating flesh will be no more;
On that day you'll enter heaven's gated door.

So Happy Birthday my dear Pastor and friend;
I pray next year the page will be turned again!

CHOSEN ONES

Thank God for Bishop and Sister Pippens, The chosen ones.
They always make sure God's work is thoroughly done.

Thank God for the chosen ones.

They set the example of what a saint is to be.
Thank God they are praying for me.

My goal is to go to heaven one day.
Thank God they are showing me the way.

Thank God for the chosen ones.

They are so precious to me.
Thank God for their light I can see.

Oh thank God for the chosen ones.

So as I end this song of love.
May God bless you both from heaven above.

Thank God for the chosen ones.
Oh thank God for the chosen ones.

Monica

Monica, can be a lawyer, a doctor, a nurse, or whatever she wants to be;
She must have a vision a dream that she can see.

Monica, is caring and she is also kind;
She is strong in mind.

Monica I truly believe in you;
There are so many great things you can do.

Hold your head up and stand tall;
You are somebody, you do count and God loves you most of all.

Someone

Someone who is loving and kind.
Someone who helps when you are in a bind.

Someone who serves the Lord 100%.
Someone who listens when you need to vent.

Someone who knows the Word inside and out.
Someone who presents the Word that makes you shout!

Someone who is a wonderful husband and father.
Someone who always says, "Oh you're no bother."

Someone who is always available for a baptismal dippin'.
This someone is our very own, Thank God, Elder
Anthony Pippens.

GOD'S GIFT OF POETRY

THE ULTIMATE

As I read your wonderful writings;
I sensed an abundance of frustration, pain and emotional fighting.

Seeking your place in life, waiting to be the ultimate man, strong and assured with a feeling of accomplishment;
Fighting the pain of the things of the past, yet overcoming obstacles of time present.

Seeking for the ultimate love that will lift you when you're down, create a smile from a frown, give support when hope seems lost and a gentle touch;
Doesn't anyone hear you, can't they see, are you asking for too much?

Wanting to throw your hands up in the air;
A gesture of giving up because of a feeling no one cares.

Dear one, because I stand on the outside I can tell you what I perceive;
You are a loving, protecting father of three.

You are kind, caring, with concern for others;
You help and respect your fellow brothers.

Your strength is projected from the inside out;
Your shoulders pulled back as a man with great clout.

You come to church to worship the Lord, raising your arms with outstretched hands;
Being obedient and a God fearing man.

GOD'S GIFT OF POETRY

I just wanted to let you know, that ultimate love, the
hope in life, the healing of time past and present miseries,
and that gentle touch, well you have had them all along,
they were never lost;

For the Great and Gracious King of glory gave all these
things to you when he died on the cross.

Keep on being the outstanding person you are;
And know, with God's grace you can go far.

THE VISION

Elder, you have a vision given to you from the Lord;
and you know with God nothing is too hard.

You have diligently worked and sought the Master's will;
Because of your obedience, hard work, compassion, love,
and faithfulness, your vision will be fulfilled.

Some people have been cruel, cold and mean;
Some are jealous for they have no vision to be seen.

But God is embracing you because of your trust;

Romans 8:37 says *Nay in all things we are more than conquers through him that loved us.*

Because of your vision, many souls, will be won;
God is blessing you, my dear pastor for a spiritual job well done.

A FLOWER

A flower is created by the Lord above;
So beautiful bright in color and radiating His love.

They stand tall in the strong breeze of a wind;
From God's strength they only bend.

They are beautiful within and without;
Such a wonderful gift from God, without a doubt.

I say this to say, Angie, you are a flower that stands tall;
God loves you and you have heard His call.

You are a ray of sunshine your inner light shines through;
I do thank JESUS for flowers like you.

Matt 5:16 *Let your light so shine before men, that they may see your good works, and glorify your Father which is in-heaven.*

OUR BELOVED

So thoughtful and caring, so faithful, so persistent and daring;
Holding on when their cup is full.

Loving and kind concerned about all;
Reaching out and lifting up those that fall.

Lending their ear to their sadness, anger, and fear;
Always setting God's example, they are so dear.

Always elevating and glorifying God above;
Reaching out extending God's love.

A team on that is truly on the Lord's side;
God is in the midst of their marital ties.

Their light glows bright as that of a precious jewel;
Being generated by the Holy Ghost fuel.

They are truly God's chosen ones;
He knew they would get his work done.

GOD'S GIFT OF POETRY

Conclusion

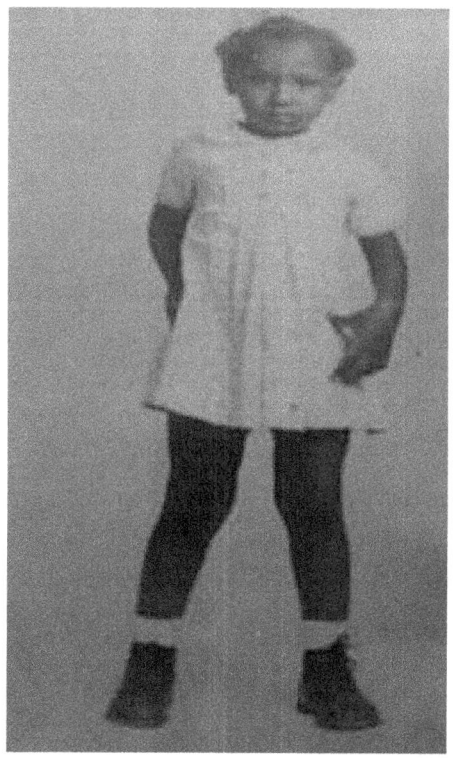

Little girl running and playing, she had such a great imagination. She really didn't want her picture taken as you probably can tell. She loved taking care of people. She wanted to be a nurse when she grew up. She loved animals of all kinds and still does.

She had two little chickens that followed her everywhere she went, their names was Mike and Ike. She would play so hard every day riding her horsey which was a broom stick up and down the hills in the pasture. She would chase the bad guys and shoot them with her little cap gun.

She loved being in the pasture with the cows. She would even lick the block of salt with the cows. yuk! She began to get older and would go to Sunday School. This is where she heard about Jesus because of her great imagination, she always looked in the sky wanting and hoping to see Jesus. She would pray hard asking Jesus to please let her see him.

She was always playing like she was a nurse. She had her toy doctor's bag her dear mother bought. She believed she healed everyone. This little girl grew up and now she sees Jesus every day, you see she accepted Him in her life and guess what, she also became a nurse doing what she loved to do, taking care of people and loving them. She was nominated Nurse of the Year, imagine that! Well you just never know how things are going to turn out. I can truly say thank you Jesus!

Maria Tipton

                May God bless you.

The Infinite Wonder

I woke up this morning with a great desire to write about my Lord and Savior Jesus Christ and share it with you. I really don't know what you think of him or if you even have any thought of him at all but I am here to tell you of his greatness in my life.

As I reflect back on my life, which was in shambles. I can truly say if it was not for the Lord I would not be where I am today. I remember as a child I always wanted to see Jesus. I would look into the sky and pray he would let me see him.*Little did I know at that time he was always there for me. I was not in a place in my life to really understand. I went to Sunday School so I had some idea who he was. It is so very important to bring your children up in church. The bible says *"to bring up a child in the way he should go and when her is old he shall not depart from it."* **Proverbs 6:23**. I have seen Jesus many times and I don't mean seeing him in actual body but in spirit through his working.

One day Jesus sent a witness to me who told me Jesus loved me and wanted me to be saved. You see Jesus doesn't make us do anything. Don't misunderstand me, he is all power and he can do whatever he wants. In **Genesis 1:1** it says **"In the beginning God created the heavens and the earth."** Remember in **Exodus** chapter **14** when God parted the Red Sea for the Israelites when Pharaoh was after them to kill them? He is an awesome and powerful God. He gives us a choice

I accepted the call of my Savior in 1986 and I can tell you my life was totally changed. Before I became saved I was abused by the world. No matter what I did, I was never satisfied. I have four children and I know I could have given them a better life. I answered the call of Jesus to be saved. I believed in him and was baptized in Jesus name and received the Holy Spirit. I then became a new creature like the Bible says in **2 Corinthians 5:17**. I didn't want to do the things of the past anymore. I was 44 years old when I got baptized.

My pastor told me I didn't have to worry about those cigarettes anymore. I honestly thought in my mind, how I had tried to quit many times but could not and now the desire is gone? I couldn't comprehend what he was saying to me.

I am here to tell you I have not had cigarettes or drugs since I came up out of the water of baptism, a new creature. It is just as God said in **2 Corinthians 5:17**. God cleaned me up just as he said. My life is so wonderful now.

The Bible speaks about having the faith of a mustard seed in **Matthew 17** verse **20** * Jesus has taught me how to do this. In **Philippians 4:13** it says *"I can do all things through Christ which strengthened me."*

There are all kinds of concerns in these days and times we are living in.

People are accepting and doing whatever makes them feel good. My heart goes out to the people who refuse to know believe and claim the Lord Savior Jesus Christ in their lives, I was once one of those persons, so I can tell you, you are being deceived. The Bible tells us in **1stCorinthians 6:9-10**. *Know ye not that the unrighteous shall not inherit the kingdom of God? Be not deceived; neither fornicators, nor idolaters nor adulterers, nor effeminate, nor abusers of themselves with mankind,10 Nor thieves, nor covetous nor drunkards, nor revilers, nor extortioners, shall Inherit the kingdom of God.*

I used to be depressed all the time no sense of hope just darkness in my life. Since I have been saved I have learned depression comes to one who feels lonely. It is a problem of the lost, unloved and hopeless. Since I have come to know my Jesus, he tells me the devil is a liar and the father of it. He tells me to learn to trust the Lord Jesus not my own understanding. And encourages me in all my ways to acknowledge him and he will direct my path. He is my very present help in trouble. He will never leave you nor forsake you.

Depression is now a thing of the past. If I feel depression coming on I go to the Father. He is rich in mercy and grace and love. I do as the word says, the joy of the Lord is my strength. He causes all of these scriptures to come to mind and I am peaceful.

It just doesn't matter what you are going through The Bible says, *is there anything too hard for the Lord?* He created the universe, and created man out of the dust of the ground. He blew into him the breath of life, and He parted the Red Sea. The Israelites were in the wilderness for 40 years yet their clothing never wore out. The same can be said for their shoes. They never went hungry because God fed them manna from heaven and quail.

The Bible says, Jesus is the same yesterday and today and forever. I am telling you now, Jesus is waiting for you so won't you surrender to him and remove yourself from the bondage of the devil. Then you will finally be set free. The devil wants you to die and go to hell with him. God wants you to have life and that more abundantly.

Come to Jesus Christ today

GOD'S GIFT OF POETRY

About The Author

Maria Tipton was born in Brazil, Indiana. She moved to Indianapolis in 1966. She is the mother of five children, Gregory Rhodes, Jeffery Rhodes (deceased), Gena Landers, Lisa Savage and Bridgette Montgomery. She has many grandchildren and great-grandchildren. She graduated from Indianapolis Public School of Practical Nursing in 1977. She was nominated Nurse of the Year in 1988 at St Francis Hospital in the Obstetric Department. She accepted Christ in her life in 1986. She is married to a wonderful man of God, Elder Robert M. Tipton Jr. She is currently an Evangelist doing what she was created to do. She lives to glorify God in every aspect of her life. God has blessed her with the gift of poetry.

GOD'S GIFT OF POETRY

Index

Chapter 1

Page 18..Contrary
Page 20...Free
Page 21......................................He Is Risen
Page 23..Seeking
Page 24..The King
Page 26..Woman

Chapter 2

Page 28......................................A Year By Grace
Page 30..Comforter
Page 31...Heaven
Page 32......................................Running Child
Page 33...........................Matters Of The Heart
Page 34......................................The Suffering
Page 36..Farewell

Chapter 3

Page 38..He Who
Page 40..Life
Page 41...Love

Chapter 4

Page 43..Awakened
Page 44...Eternal
Page 45...Forgiveness
Page 46...Hatred
Page 47..Mercy
Page 48...Motivation

Chapter 5

Page 50........................Question & Answers
Page 52...................................Rock A Bye
Page 53..................................Secret Place
Page 54...Soldier
Page 55......................................The Flesh
Page 56..The Key
Page 57.....................................The Stand
Page 58........................The Very Same One
Page 59....................................Tomorrow
Page 60..............................Mother's Love

Chapter 6

Poems of Personal Encouragement
Page 62..................Love Letter To My Children
Page 63..Mother
Page 64...TKC
Page 65.................................The Beginning
Page 67...A Light

Page 68..Appreciate
Page 69..First Lady
Page 70..Message
Page 71..Shouldn't Be
Page 72..Alexis
Page 73..Another Year
Page 74..Chosen Ones
Page 75..Monica
Page 76..Someone
Page 77..The Ultimate
Page 79..The Vision
Page 80..A Flower
Page 81..Our Beloved

GOD'S GIFT OF POETRY

GOD'S GIFT OF POETRY

www.ingramcontent.com/pod-product-compliance
Lightning Source LLC
Chambersburg PA
CBHW072023060426
42449CB00034B/1878